Raphael N. Luzon was born in Benghazi in 1954. He studied Political Science at the University of Roma, International Relations at Oxford University, and worked in public diplomacy for sixteen years. He was also a correspondent in Italy and Israel, working for *Maariv*, *Hadashot*, Radio Galei Zahal and RAI Italian TV. He currently resides in London and works as a freelance journalist and analyst, specializing in the Middle East.

Raphael Luzon

Libyan Twilight

The Story of an Arab Jew

Introduced by Roberto Saviano

DARF PUBLISHERS, LONDON

This edition first published in UK 2016
By DARF PUBLISHERS LTD
277 West End Lane
London
NW6 1QS
United Kingdom

Copyright © Darf Publishers 2016

First published in Italian by Giuntina 2015 as *Tramonto
libico: Storia di un ebreo arabo* by Raphael Luzon

Translated by Gaia Luzon
The moral right of the author has been asserted

All rights reserved
This book is sold subject to the condition that it shall not,
by way of trade or otherwise, be lent, resold, hired out, or
otherwise circulated without the publisher's prior consent
in any form of binding or cover other than that in which it
is published and without a similar condition, including this
condition, being imposed on the subsequent purchaser.

Cover designed by Luke Pajak

ISBN-13: 978-1-85077-298-9
eBook ISBN-13: 978-1-850-77-299-6

Printed by Mega Printing in Turkey

In memory of the Luzon & Raccah families massacred in June 1967, and all the Jews buried in Libya. I also dedicate this book to Sir Martin Gilbert (1936–2015) for his outstanding contribution to Arab Jewish history.

'In a place where there are no men, strive to be a man.'
Ethics of the Fathers 2:5

'I am not born for any one corner of the universe; this whole world is my country.'
Seneca

Acknowledgements

I first thank God who allowed me to reach this point. The production of *Libyan Twilight* would not have been possible without the support and belief from Darf Publishers' Director, Ghassan Fergiani. I'm also thankful to my friend Khaeri Giuma Abushagor for all the encouragement, and giving me the final push. A special thank you to Roberto Saviano for his interest and contribution to the book with his insightful Introduction, and to all my friends and family for their patience and continuous support, particularly: Ahmed Rahal, Ghazi Gheblawi, Abdallah Al Kebir, Majdulein Abaida and the thousands of followers on Facebook. I will be forever grateful to my daughter Gaia for her translation of *Libyan Twilight* from the Italian, and Deborah Sherer for her editorial work on the text. Without all of you this project wouldn't have been possible.

Insights, photographs, videos and documents covering the events of this book, can be found on:

www.rluzon.net

Introduction

Official estimates speak of about 856,000 Jews who have fled their homes, cities and countries. Some Jews refer to themselves as 'Arab Jews' because Arabic was their language, and for centuries, if not millennia, their roots were in the land of sun, desert and sea ranging from the Middle East to the Maghreb. Iraq, Syria, Iran, Lebanon, Tunisia, Morocco, Egypt, Algeria, Yemen, Tunisia, Aden, Libya: countries that had large, flourishing Jewish communities, formed by merchants, craftsmen, rabbis, scholars, doctors and administrators. Communities of 30,000 to 150,000 Jews who no longer exist, crashed into exile following the persecution and discrimination mounted after 1948, the birth of the State of Israel.

This book tells one of these stories, that of the Libyan Jews. It is assumed that the first Jews arrived in the territory once known as the Barbary Coast, which was inhabited by *barbaroi* (what the Greeks called those who didn't speak their language), after the destruction of the First Temple, Jerusalem, in 586 bc.

From then until 1967, the year in which *Libyan Twilight* begins, Jews have contested each new conqueror in North Africa. They fought with the Berbers against the armies of Mohammed, contributed to the growth of the region during the Ottoman Empire and Italian colonisation and mixed with the local population. However, they have always maintained their own traditions and a strong bond with their ancient faith. To understand the compliancy of the Jews of Libya, we can look to the Fascist era, when three Jews were publicly flogged after refusing to keep their stores open during Shabbat. At the beginning of the 1900s, there were no less than forty-four synagogues in Tripoli, indicating a fervent Jewish life and a deeply religious community.

Fascism carried the shame of racial laws. On 18 March 1937, Mussolini landed in Tripoli to declare: 'Italy considers the Jews to be under her protection. There is no racial or religious discrimination in my mind, remaining true to the policy of equality in the eyes of the law and freedom of worship.' In July of the following year, he published the infamous 'Manifesto of Race' that sanctioned discrimination against Jews by labelling them as inferior to the Muslim population. With the outbreak of World War II in 1939, around three thousand Jews were detained in a prison camp and three men accused of collaborating with the British were shot dead. This discrimination lasted until General Montgomery landed at Calabria, with the allies liberating Libya from the Italians shortly after.

Nevertheless, this liberation didn't establish a new period of peace for the Libyan Jews. The rise of Zionism and the strengthening of pan-Islamism emitted latent and destructive energies that brooded in the recesses of the Arab masses and resulted in repeated pogroms and attacks on Jewish neighbourhoods. In 1967, the Six Day War broke out. This angered Arabs and led to the expulsion of the Libyan Jews, ending a history that had lasted more than two thousand years.

In a sincere manner, Raphael Luzon reflects on the past, but he is aware that memory is deceptive and therefore he cannot claim to assert the absolute truth, nor is it an instrument that serves ideological impulses. It seems to me that Luzon has opened a big can of memories primarily for therapeutic purposes, to soothe the wounds of exile and to give relief to the nostalgia for his homeland; a nostalgia that lives between the lines of *Libyan Twilight*.

The author's other motivation is the pursuit of justice. We learn about the assassination of the Luzon and Raccah families in Tripoli, a crime that never resulted in a trial or conviction; nor was there a funeral for the innocent victims. Without anger or a desire for revenge, Luzon seeks justice.

I was impressed with Luzon's openness when dealing with others and his deep desire for reconciliation and dialogue between different religions, a dialogue that relies on equality. I then discovered that Luzon's political activities for the preservation of Libyan Jewry continues to this day in a fervent confrontation between Jews, Muslims and Christians, who refuse to surrender to extremism.

Libyan Twilight is a short book, which is well written and can be read very quickly. I recommend you linger, keep it with you for a while, leafing back and rereading sections, because, in the words of Luzon, we can often find the inspiration to embark on a path of peace and memory.

Roberto Saviano

Chapter One

I had long since lost track of time. They'd taken everything from me, even my watch. The Saharan heat permeated through window cracks, further oppressing the cell's silence, only to be interrupted by a barking dog in the distance. I was all alone with my thoughts and the whimpering of prisoners being tortured and interrogated elsewhere. The thought of death was surprisingly calming; my only worries were about my wife, daughter and two sisters.

The cell was empty, with decaying graffiti-filled walls, and the stench of urine and mould permeating the room. The only item in there was a tattered brown leather armchair that stood in the corner. I was finding it hard to sit for long, so I'd pace continually to remain sane. I'd fall asleep for only a couple of minutes at a time, awakened by memories of places and half-forgotten faces. How painful it was that the only thing keeping me awake was feeling guilty about my fam-ily! The thoughts dried up in my throat as I squeezed my eyes shut in fear and apprehension. This time I had gone too far in my desperate optimism. My faith in fellowship, coex-istence, forgiveness and the triumph of good over evil was rolling away.

Why was I in a Benghazi prison in the scorching Libyan summer? I questioned myself, leaning my forehead against the clammy wall, with the constant urge to cry, but remain-ing tearless. How well I knew the people and their propensity for violence. It takes a lone leaf to break away off a branch and hit the ground; everything can change from love to hate, from prayers to curses and from life to death. I had seen everything and forgotten nothing in Libya, the land where I was born.

Chapter Two

The sweet scent of aftershave clashed with the grimy smell of Shafik's barber's shop. He used to stand behind the barber's chair, cutting and trimming, or playing backgammon with customers. The whole city was familiar with this short, stubby man with his sleek hair and perfectly groomed moustache. He was a cheeky character, whose lively black eyes had a harshness, reflecting a merciless gleam at times.

It was a warm spring afternoon. A soft breeze swayed the palm trees to the rhythm of the sea. As my hair was too long, my mother yelled at me to go to Shafik's. She walked me to the door, her gaze following me until I turned the corner.

I was on Shafik's barber's chair while he was busy trimming the white beard of an elderly customer. His assistant Ahmed was engrossed in the newspaper. Standing behind me, Salvatore, an Italian immigrant from Sicily, produced a white cloth and tied it behind my neck. He then commenced cutting off big chunks of hair. There was an unusual silence in the shop. I could only hear the sound of scissors. It soothed me, along with the touch of Salvatore's hands and the aroma oozing out of the bottles beneath the mirror. I almost fell asleep in the hands of barber but the reflection in the mirror stopped me, making me think about how I'd turned adolescent.

Suddenly, Salvatore leaned very close to my ear and whispered, 'You will see, kid, soon they'll strangle all you Jews.' I froze, not comprehending what he meant. I caught Salvatore's evil look of satisfaction in the mirror. He continued cutting as if nothing had happened.

The old man next to me paid and ruefully left the shop. I sensed a compassionate look. Salvatore had finished and, as usual, Shafik strolled over to make sure the hair cut was done perfectly – more of a habit than attention to detail. Brushing off the last strands of hair with precise gestures, Salvatore said in a gentle tone, 'You Jews, it seems your days are numbered'. His glance suggested that I shouldn't worry. I knew that being a Jew in Libya meant being resented by some. Ahmed's voice, from behind his paper, immediately triggered my sense of fear.

'Leave the boy alone...'

Shafik loosened the cloth around my neck and shook it free in dramatic fashion, strewing my shorn hair on the floor. I looked at them for a few seconds as if they had something to reveal me.

'Well?' Shafik said. I handed over the dinars to him and swiftly left the shop. I started running, faster and faster, until I reached my front door, out of breath.

'What happened, son?' my mother asked as soon as she opened the door. I simply embraced her, as I had nothing to say.

Chapter Three

Benghazi, 4 June 1967

Zaineb, so slow yet so efficient. Your gestures were so careful and considered. So intricate, like a panther stalking its prey. We sometimes watched you in fascination. In the late after-noon you returned to your shack, leaving our house spotless, a sanctuary without a trace of dust or grime. While working, you sang quietly. Alone in a room, you sang fearlessly. Your songs were essentially Libyan blues, much like the songs of American slaves, who sang the stories of suffering. Your black skin glowed like all those from the Fezzan region.

You lived in the shanty town on the outskirts of Benghazi, an area in dire condition. My mother gave you old dresses, some food and money before you left the house. We didn't know much about you, as you never wanted to tell us any-thing. No emotions were present on your face, and your eyes never gave away anything. You always looked at us with such love and affection. You were a good nanny, even though you enjoyed scaring us for fun. We would jump with fright, but your generous smile spread across your face and your hands embraced us with love.

You have protected me from my father's temper. Also, you were the only one who made my sister Betty eat until she cleared her plate. Betty used to obey you.

That particular night, our house was as immaculate as ever. Once again you surprised us with the magic of your care. You were ready to leave after placing the brooms and mops back in the cupboard. You walked up to me, knelt down and embraced me for a long time. Next was my sister Betty, before giving a kiss to little Rita. You went into the study to say goodbye to my father, squeezing his hand. You'd never done this before. Finally, you approached my mother and hugged her tightly. It seemed as if you wouldn't let her go. I was standing in front of you watching your tears stream down your cheeks onto your shoulders.

My mother freed herself from Nanny's embrace. 'What's wrong, Zaineb?' she asked worriedly. You lowered your gaze, unable to reply as you left the house, forgetting to close the door.

The next day, none of the servants who cleaned the homes of Jewish families returned to work. None except you, Zaineb. You worked as usual, then wept and left for your shack, to your life, without saying a word.

Lailat al-maal Kippur. Yom Kippur Eve. A night of expiation before the Day of Atonement. In the Jewish quarter, Rabbi Madar and the teacher Rifali, who was also the kosher butcher of the community, walked from house to house. The Jewish families would wait patiently. Even the young children were awake, screaming with excitement. The chickens that my father had chosen carefully from the market felt their doom drawing closer, clucking nervously.

In front of the big synagogue, Sla al-Kabira, the voices of Jews in prayer rose in the air. Rabbi Labi would take a chicken by its neck for the ritual, Dawar Al-Ras, spinning it around my mother's head several times. Betty closed her eyes in fear when it was spun above her head, followed by Rita's. The Rabbi then tightened his grip around the chicken's neck and circled it over my father and me. The women ululated in the deafening zgaret, like a flock of birds.

'Tizkùleshanimrabbòt, Akbaldaiiar!' May you live for many years, we'd wish each other at the end of the ritual.

Rifali performed the Shechita, the kosher butchering. My mother begins the haccianifuacciaarish, purification of the chickens. The excitement rises, our sins drowned, and remorse is to follow. The whole city was looking forward to a silent and bright morning as sunrise drew closer.

Chapter Four

My footsteps echoed in the silence of the city's great cathedral as I passed the building and the confession rooms, brushing against the hallway walls that led to the middle school, Giovanni XXIII. The Franciscan fathers and the Italian consulate of Benghazi waited, as it was end-of-year exams.

Although I was well prepared, I felt anxious, as if my memory would miraculously be erased. We pupils were always smartly dressed on important occasions, sitting up straight. Both Jews and gentiles, we had our sweaty palms clasped as we waited. Eventually, the envelopes containing our exam papers were opened.

An hour later, the doors of the hall opened and Father Anselmo, pale, sweat-drenched and breathless, entered. He and I shared a similar passion: radio. Sometimes he would give me a lift home in his car and we'd chat about our common interest. I smiled as he entered the room, almost forgetting the exam papers in front of me.

However, soon the room was filled with the clamorous voices, loud explosions, car horns and violent cries from outside. The smile on my face instantly disappeared as I caught Father Anselmo's anxious eyes. Everyone sensed danger, particularly the Jewish children.

The priests took us all into an office and asked us to stay silent. On the wall facing us was a large wooden cross. Father Anselmo explained that a war had broken out between Israel and the Arab countries. Demonstrations had broken out in the streets, and all Jews in Libya were at risk. His words worried me more than the tumultuous noises from outside, as I sensed we were potential victims of violence for something we played no part in.

Father Anselmo started contacting our parents. Soon, some parents arrived at school to collect their children and left without a word. The phone lines were unreliable, so it was hard to contact many families, including ours. We were isolated. Some of the priests started walking some of the children home. Betty and I waited our turn, sitting with our heads low, hands in our laps. Sharing a glance with one another, we made an immediate decision. We stood up with our hands tightly gripped and quietly left the school. We ran down the cathedral's stone path, which led us to the road.

Chapter Five

We met Khammus near the Shamash Synagogue. Everyone called Khammus 'Al Fartas', meaning 'receding hairline'. He was walking close to the wall with his head down and his short legs moving swiftly. His three young children followed him. He didn't resemble a Jew, with his muscular body, Turk-ish-style moustache over his thick lips, and gnarled strong hands. Betty and I stopped Khammus. His eyes were fixed on us, waiting for our voices, but our panicked expression was enough to explain the situation.

'If somebody stops us, don't say a word,' he instructed us. 'And if they approach you, speak only in Arabic dialect, and give your names as "Ali" and "Khadija". Now follow me.'

He continued walking close to the wall. We stopped at the nun's school to pick up Rita, our younger sister. She was waiting for us behind the gate, holding a nun's hand. We continued walking as a group. Sweaty, breathless men were running in all directions, their hands brandishing iron rods, while they cursed the Jews and Israel. Loudspeakers on top of cars were blaring out the news of Arab victory and the surrender of the Jews, announcing that Arab armies were only a few kilometres away from Tel Aviv.

We crossed Cagni Square, now known as 'Maydan al-Shajra'. A Jew, Bedussa, owned a huge textile showroom here, the biggest of its kind in Benghazi. The showroom had two en-trances and, when shut, we'd see a huge neon sign written in Arabic and Italian: 'Bedussa'. It was said that the Bedussa family were protected by the Auagir tribe, one of the most influential in Cyrenaica. Whether this was true or not, it was of no use to the Bedussa family in the midst of the violence. We witnessed a mob swarming into the showroom and set-ting it ablaze.

'Don't be frightened, children,' Khammus murmured. 'Don't run, walk slowly, as you are doing now.' He appeared calm, giving us courage and proving he was a strong man. However, it was clear that he was worried. Small mobs merged into larger mobs, shouting for the destruction of Is-rael. People were running in all directions. What had Nasser to do with anything? What had Israel to do with anything?

We realised that we were nearing home, but a Muslim stopped us saying, 'Where are you running to, Jews?' His evil grin frightened us.

'We're not running,' Khammus answered. 'We're going home.'

Again, he interrupted with his loud, laughing voice, 'Today isn't a good day for you Jews. You'd be better locking your-selves in!'

Benghazi's Municipality Square was filled with demonstrators. Jews were caught, savagely beaten, pushed to the ground and kicked. All of the Jewish stores were set on fire. The three pharmaceutical and cosmetic shops owned by my father were also set ablaze. Huge explosions broke out, since many of the products contained alcohol. Khammus picked up an iron rod from the ground and lifted his other arm to gesture to us to remain close. Now he started walking faster. Another Jew joined us, looking confused.

Finally we reached our street, but the screams and chants followed us. Running, we burst into the house and shut the door behind us. The door's standard lock offered us little protection. We dropped to the floor and huddled together, breathing heavily and waiting. Some of them started bang-ing loudly on the door, while others were shouting. The door rattled from the thumping kicks, but the mob left after a few minutes, away from our house and leaving us alive.

Chapter Six

Soon thick black smoke from the streets seeped into the houses, poisoning the air. Some of the women were vomiting, crouched over the toilets and holding on to each other. The men were praying, rushing through the words as if they wouldn't be given a chance to reach God before a massacre would strike. Some of them were crying shamelessly, as if their destiny had already been decided and we were all mourning. Khammus stood still in front of the door, holding the iron rod in his hand. I was observing his robust frame and muscular arms, and the determination on his face. His presence strengthened our confidence.

My mother cautiously stepped out of the house and knocked on the door of our Egyptian neighbour, expecting help. She soon realised they weren't home, leaving us choking, coughing, crying and praying. There were long moments filled with silence as we sat staring at the floor while the anarchy outside continued. It wasn't until evening that police sirens entered the city streets.

All of a sudden, we heard a knock on our door. We remained silent and still. No one dared go near the windows. Our lives were hanging by a thread of irrevocable judgement.

A voice commanded us to open the door in an authoritative tone. 'The demonstrators have dispersed. You have nothing to fear.' It was a police official. He explained, 'I have orders to take all the Jews to the police station for their protection.' My father didn't answer, thinking it might be a trap.

'In the name of Awad Abdeljeuad,' the official continued. He was the head of security, the *al-kawa al-motaharrika-*

(the special forces unit), and was a good friend of my father. Peeping through a small hole, we confirmed that an official and commandos were outside, so we opened the door. They entered the house while my mother watched the mob through the window, under the custody of two police officers who refused to leave. They wanted to kill us.

Chapter Seven

The police escorted us out of the house. With our heads hung low, my sisters and I walked fearfully beside our father, gripping his jacket, while the hate-filled eyes and violent chants closed in on us. It felt as if the whole of Benghazi had gathered outside our home to lynch us. I still couldn't comprehend why; it all felt like a Biblical saga, and we were being hurled into the flames of hell.

Stones flew past our heads as we clambered into the police vans, with only the clothes on our backs. The roar of the engine and tyres on the road slowly drowned out the mob as we faded into distance, still unable to comprehend the day's events.

The officers instructed us not to lift the netting on the sides of the van, but we children were compelled to disobey. Flames engulfed the Jewish shops on the streets we passed.

About three hundred of us were taken to the central police station, where we disembarked from the vans and sat together on the pavement. The police offered us tea and coffee. The aroma seemed to give us a glimmer of hope as we warmed our hands, but it was short-lived. The mob was heading towards us, as we could hear their screams getting closer.

To make matters worse, we heard the announcement on the police station's radio, by Khadija Jamie, a famous journalist, pleading with citizens to remain calm and to stop their assault on innocent people. This triggered silence, awash with panic over the impending tragedy cast over us.

Immediately, the officers instructed us to get back into the vans to be evacuated and we rushed to obey. No one questioned the instruction. Our fate was no longer in our own hands, and the idea of escaping seemed less realistic by the minute.

Chapter Eight

Soon our vehicle was moving through silent open spaces. We felt as though we left Benghazi without a final glance. Eventually, the vans came to a halt and we settled down on the dusty grounds of the Remy Army Base.

'Here you will be safe,' an official assured us. From the middle of the courtyard we were escorted to big cabins, where we found some dogs awaiting our arrival. The soldiers stood in the doorway of each cabin, and attempted to separate men from women and children. Immediately, everyone rebelled – all the women started screaming and the men refused to move. The families feared being separated. So we raised our heads and demanded our rights, for the first time, and to our great relief the officials obliged.

We had nothing to eat, only a cup of tea. Mothers were holding their young ones in front of them as the rest of us waited behind. Not one single person thought about sleep. Murmurings began to grow louder as people debated possibilities. Most of us were convinced we'd been taken there to be killed.

News arrived the next morning along with the sunrise. 'It is impossible for you people to go back to Benghazi,' the commander explained. 'The situation is too tense there, and your lives are in danger. For the moment you'll stay put.'

We were given some blankets as well as some groceries, like rice, flour, bread and potatoes. Women started cooking and organising things as well as they could. Although our hearts were filled with fear, signs of normality began to float back into our lives. When they asked us if we'd like to have some meat, we had to make sure it was kosher. Rabbi Madar, who was also a *shochet*, butchered chickens in a corner of the courtyard. The men of the community gathered round to block the scene from the view of the women and children. That corner became the are a assigned to kosher butchering. No violent or distressing sights were seen around kosher butchers; rather, a feeling of hope arose, in faith and eternity. The eternal feeling of God's presence, and our will to remain as Jews, regardless of the situation.

Chapter Nine

Some of the men were secretly listening to the BBC in a corner of a cabin. I could sense their fear, as I stood behind my father. There was a fear of being caught by the officers, but even stronger was the anxiety of trying to fathom the outcome of the war and the fate of Israel. Soon we discovered that there was no news of assassination and surrender.

Six days later, the Egyptian, Jordanian and Syrian armies had been routed and all of Jerusalem was held by the Israelis. The youngest people cheered, some cried with joy, but the adults ordered us to remain calm, not to show any signs of happiness, fearing retaliation by the military. We all kept the relief, euphoria and satisfaction buried within ourselves. My father took my hand and squeezed it until it hurt, a grip of redemption and renewed hope. For the first time ever, he picked me up and held me close.

Two officials then arrived at our cabin and instructed us to gather in the main courtyard. The commander arrived briskly, with his hair slicked back and wearing a well-pressed uniform. He spat his words in haste without looking at us, and instead stared into the horizon above our heads. Summarising the events of the recent days, he mentioned the danger of returning to Benghazi. Then he made a statement that decided the end of our lives – a few words that superseded two thousand years of history, leaving us all paralysed: 'There is no other choice than to leave Libya.'

We were only allowed to take one suitcase and twenty Libyan pounds with us to Italy. Two members of each family would return in secrecy to Benghazi to collect clothes and personal belongings from their homes. My father requested permission to take as much medicine as possible from his pharmacy as an investment.

How should one react to the destruction of an entire community? Some were embracing, others crying; some were walking aimlessly around the courtyard while others returned to the cabins. Families gathered together in small groups, trying to make sense of the fate of their properties, their homes, their careers and their bank accounts. Some of them were worried about our sacred books, the synagogues and the Torah scrolls. The surge of events had left us disoriented. Everything seemed surreal, even ridiculous. Our future lay somewhere ahead in a black fog.

News of the death of a grandmother from the Zarrugh family rippled through our community. She couldn't bear leaving her country, her Benghazi, in for another country.

She was the last of our community to be buried in Benghazi's Jewish Cemetery. Rabbi Madar and a few others were escorted by Libyan army personnel to Benghazi, where they recited the Kaddish not only for Grandmother Zarrugh, but for our whole community, which died on the same day.

We were frustrated with the lack of news from Tripoli, which was also home to a large Jewish community. My father's mother, two brothers and two sisters were there, along with their own families. The officials vaguely replied to our anguished inquiries, but to our despair there was no way of finding out the extent of the situation. Arguments erupted for no apparent reason, and some of the men became violent. However, these short outbreaks always ended in an anxious silence tinged with guilt. Nevertheless, we remained brothers and everything was soon forgotten. By the time of evening prayers, we were once again united as one family.

One morning, a few of my father's Muslim customers turned up, most of whom were pharmacists. Among them, only a few paid their debts immediately, while others openly refused, giving the reason that we were leaving Libya, which they believed was a good enough reason not to settle the payments.

Haj Ayad Barruin, owner of a pharmacy in the city of Bayda, travelled to our camp despite the risks. He shook his head insistently and promised to 'help' us by purchasing all of our property in Benghazi.

He promised he would send money to Rome once we arrived, a sum that was half the real value of all our property. A few weeks later, however, we received only 5 percent of what he had promised and we never heard from him again. Haj Ayad Barruin had appropriated everything my parents had worked hard for all those years.

And so we left Libya, bereft and dispossessed, leaving behind our deceased relatives and our homes. We boarded the plane with broken hearts, questioning whether we would ever see our country again. Our home!

Being a child, I felt a sense of relief leaving behind all that violence: the horrific sounds of screaming, the fire, and all the hate I had witnessed. Although I wasn't happy, my anxiety momentarily lifted as I found myself in a new place, with a sweet and soothing feeling that after all I was, and we all were, still alive. Now I hoped there was the possibility of a better future. Despite the grief-stricken faces of my parents, Betty, Rita and I looked through the plane's porthole and were fascinated at the clear skies that stretched to the horizon. The sound of the muezzin was now behind us, and the sonorous bells of Rome lay ahead.

On the first day of the month of Nisan my mother used to make bsisa, a traditional dish made by Libyan Jews to commemorate the day the Mishkin (tabernacle) was erected. Her swollen fingers kneaded the flour vigorously. Her body was bent over the bowl, her sleeves rolled up, her eyes fixated on the pastry, as she worked her arms tirelessly until it started to take shape. The ingredients are flour, coriander, cumin, almonds, dried fruits, dates and sugar. Once everything was mixed, she would insert small trinkets, including at least one key. Before tasting this traditional dish we'd pray to God saying, 'Yafetchah, Bla Neftchah, Yaatai, Blamenai, Arzikna war zikmana!' (God, you are the one who can open without keys, always giving a generous hand, giving without compensation. Giving us your goodness so that we can do good to others!) There is no rejuvenation without bsisa; the sacrament is incomplete without this delicious bsisa, as old as the dawn of time. I used to watch my busy mother preparing the meal. She would turn and smile at me and offer her finger to taste the sweet paste. She would laugh as I licked it and continue kneading, going into her own little world.

Chapter Ten

We disembarked at Rome airport with heavy hearts, despite the fact that we were now safe. We were now immigrants, and the only belongings relating to our past life was the meagre luggage we carried with us. A group of Libyan Jews awaited us at the terminal. Among them were Raffaello Fellah, Mimmo Uzan and Dori Zard, plus other representatives of the Jewish community and the humanitarian organisation, Joint. We were directed to a bus, where all the children instantly dropped from exhaustion and the adults were dishevelled and confused.

A man boarded the bus trying to encourage us with words of hope. He continued over a microphone, saying that this was the beginning of a new era, since we had left the enemies to their destinies, and our community was safe now and we would rebuild our lives in Rome, a big city with many Jews. We listened, but the words drew tears, even as we tried to suppress them. There's nothing worse than trying to cheer someone suffering from loss. Our unknown brother, despite his best intentions, failed to rouse an ounce of enthusiasm. He tried to make us sing. '*Hevenu shalom alechem, hevenu shalom alechem...,*' he chimed while clapping with his free hand. But no one followed. Some watched him curiously and most showed displeasure.

Finally, a scream arose from the far end of the bus: 'Enough!' We all began laughing hysterically, easing the tension.

We believed that our destination was Rome, but soon we realised that we were being transported to a camp in Capua,

about 25 km north of Napoli. But we were too tired to pro-
test or question it. We let ourselves be taken away like a bottle in the sea, drifting at the mercy of the winds and waves.
Our only hope was our ancient faith.

My Father

My father's name was Amos, but we used to call him Mamus, sometimes Quintino. He was the youngest of eight brothers, and grew up in a healthy family with solid values. He studied at both the Italian and rabbinical school. Once done with their homework, he and his brothers used to help their father, who was a dealer in cattle and spices. This made him a strong, decisive man, which eventually led to him running a company importing pharmaceuticals and establishing various warehouses to provide goods for all of Cyrenaica.

We had servants and they loved our father. He treated them with respect and generosity, often augmenting their pay. They called him *Arfi*, the Commander. In 1963, he travelled to Italy for kidney surgery. Our servants mourned as if they had been abandoned by their benefactor and they were overjoyed when he returned. The Muslim servants expressed such love for the man that a rumour spread around the back alleys of the city: Mamus had converted to Islam and had just returned from his pilgrimage to Mecca.

I loved helping him organise the warehouses and shops, carefully placing the products on shelves. I was proud to be entrusted with the task of collecting money from his retail clients. He would always reward me with a falafel sandwich and Libya's own Kitty Cola.

He had good relations with everyone, within the Jewish community and beyond, from peasants to aristocrats. Hassan al-Rida, the Prince of Libya, used to come to him for medicine. My father was a man of integrity and honesty, and that's why people loved him. Once a policeman suspected my father of a crime and he was dragged to the station and beaten. Later it was proved that my father was innocent, causing the police chief, the mayor of Benghazi and the perpetrator to apologise to my father.

People considered him as a treasurer among the Jewish community. Adding to this, he was also the *Chazan*, the Jewish cantor. He loved to sing, whether at the synagogue or at home. He would always have a melody on his lips, either humming to himself or singing out loud. Often they were liturgical tunes, sometimes they were popular Arabic songs of the time, like those sung by Farid el-Atrache, his favourite singer. He was a devoutly religious person and held a vast historical knowledge close to his heart, dating back to the expulsion during the Spanish Inquisition. To me, it seemed my father was capable of seeing reality through the eyes of his ancient ancestors.

Even though he was strict, he never raised his hands to us. He was never physically affectionate towards us, but his reassuring presence and warm tone always filled us with love. There's no doubt he was perceived as a 'great man' in our homeland, Libya.

Exile broke him. The economic and social decline, the polarity of life between Libya and Italy, demolished his existence. The mourning for a lost life never left him, so he remained what he had always been – a Libyan Jew. He took good care of us, and he worked hard to give us a good life and a future. I felt that the man I had admired all these years had left his soul in Benghazi, and I would never see the same spirit again.

In Italy he haggled over goods as he used to in Libya, but locals would mock him as he tried to be funny. The jokes he cracked fell on deaf ears and would rarely receive so much as a giggle. All his time was spent with Libyans, both Jews and Muslims. Every time he heard someone had arrived in Rome from Libya, he was filled with an in comprehensible expectation and happiness. He would try every possible way to get in touch with them so that he could hear about the situation in Libya. Not even once had he expressed his rancour or revenge towards the Libyans; he felt that fate was the culprit, responsible for everything. The situation eventually changed into degradation and then to depression. After his soul surrendered, his body followed and soon he became ill with kidney failure. Apart from a brief stint in employment, he refused to work. Once a man of wealth, he never would have thought about standing in line at the soup kitchen with charity coupons to get meals for himself and his family. My mother urged him to fight back, but her words fell on deaf ears. He had long ago lost the will to live. When he sang the prayers in the synagogue during the holidays, those were his few moments of happiness, but they didn't last long.

We were shocked to see him in such a depressed state after becoming a refugee. The news we received from Libya only made the situation worse, including my father's health. We were informed that my father's brother and our extended family in Tripoli had been murdered by a Libyan official.

A few days later Mamus needed dialysis, and his life came to an end in 1994. Mourned by the Libyan community, he was buried in Jerusalem. Despite the wounds, he never blamed the Muslims. Now I realised why he didn't allow the resentment to take over his heart. This was the only legacy he could leave me: 'The way we judge others is precisely the way he judges us.'

My Mother

My mother Rachel, whose world was shattered in the winter of 1943, had already experienced the collapse of a family, so she reacted better than my father.

She often narrated the story of an adventurous Jew in the early 1800s, who left Vienna for papal Rome, subsequently travelling to Tunis (then under French rule) to work as a courier. During this trip, he survived a shipwreck and reached a fishing village, with a small Jewish population, on the Tunisian coast. He was nicknamed 'Rumani' as he had arrived from Rome. He fell in love with a young Jewish woman, which led to him quitting his post and marrying her. The couple had a son, Benjamin Rumani, my grandfather, in 1882.

During World War II, the Allies bombed Nazi forces in the Middle East, including parts of Tunisia. One day the Allied planes appeared in the sky over the fishing village. The poor Jews were unaware of the trap, so they went outside their homes to cheer enthusiastically. The planes drew closer, gliding over their heads, and suddenly the euphoria exploded in smoke and fire as shells dropped on Tunis, killing more than a hundred Jewish civilians, including my grandmother and her children (one daughter and two sons). Another son had to have his arm amputated. From then on, every year my mother used to visit the graves of her relatives in Tunis. The trip had always filled her with unhappiness. She'd would isolate herself from us, but only for a few hours. She always recovered rapidly and returned to her natural state – a caring, affectionate mother.

These horrific memories were internalised, allowing her to be more resilient than my father. I realised women are stronger than men, and are better at handling pain. After that incident, her anxiety increased. Her eyes always watched us with apprehension, following us until we had turned the corner of our street.

In Rome she supported our family with all her love, never allowing discouragement, hatred or resentment to overcome us, despite having lost everything. In the beginning, she was our salvation, but eventually the depth of events and of life itself drowned her. When my sisters and I became independent adults, she fell into a depression and became housebound. For Betty, Rita and me to return home from school, university or work and to find our parents shut up in the flat, always in shadows and silence, was a pain that battered our souls. This seemed to be a gene that we had inherited and that would follow us for generations to come. The burden of being refugees had fallen on our parents' shoulders. For us, there was still the future with all its possibilities. We were the only blessing of their broken hearts.

Chapter Eleven

The filthy refugee camp at Capua, our first stop in Italy, also housed Eastern European and other refugees. Soon we discovered drunkards, thieves, prostitutes and vagrants among them. We were assigned a dormitory with cots, chairs and a table. The public toilets emanated a stench that haunts me to this very day. From the beginning we stuck together, without venturing through the paved alleys of the camp. In Capua, we found other Libyan Jews who had fled Tripoli. My father desperately inquired what had happened to his brother and the extended family, but found no answers. The Tripoli Jews informed him that there had been assassinations, perhaps dozens of deaths, but no one had seen his family or knew what had happened. My father did not give up and posed the same questions to all who arrived from the Libyan capital. The answers were the same. He stopped questioning once he realised that there was no one left to ask.

In those days we children were completely free, with no school and no schedule. We played all day, always having plenty of fun. However, it was only fun on the surface. Our souls were shaken, and our eyes were averted from the degradation of the surroundings.

After the first few days I began spending more and more time on my own, lying on my bed with my eyes fixed on the dormitory ceiling. For the first time, I began to dwell on images of my past life in Benghazi. It was the first time I ever experienced a sense of loss, which I was unable to express. I thought of La Salle school, my classmates and teachers. I wondered if they were thinking of me, if anybody missed me.

Memories of daily life in Benghazi appeared in my mind, people that I had never before paid attention to, but now for some reason they appeared in my reveries.

The butcher Abdullah, a Muslim who provided kosher meat, used to spend so much time with *Mashgiach* (the community's kosher food supervisor) that he'd sing the Hebrew psalms. Even though he didn't understand the lyrics, he'd still sing them continuously.

Mansour was a Muslim gentleman who spent every Shabbat evening passing through Jewish homes, switching off the lights, as Shabbat didn't permit us to do so. To thank him, everyone offered him a glass of wine. We'd often find him in the morning, drunk on the side walk.

I remembered the Jewish children running out in the streets on Purim Day, shouting, 'A' laila lilas Burim laila harfa all'amselmin!' (Tonight is Purim, a terrible night for the Muslims!), which was nothing more than paraphrasing what our Muslim friends shouted on the evening of the feast of the birth of the Prophet.

I remembered an incident that happened at school involving our Arabic teacher, Ahmed al-Sharif. Once he hit my hand with a ruler because I had apparently told a lie. He thought I had instigated a fight, but I had no involvement. With a tearful eye and a bleeding hand, I told my mother, who instantly took me to the headmaster. She began shouting and showed him my hand, insisting that the teacher should never repeat it. Ahmed al-Sharif apologised, and from then on we had an excellent relationship.

Now my sisters and I were in our beds, waiting for a goodnight kiss from our mother, waiting to fall asleep with the last thoughts of the day vanishing into the darkness of our shared room.

I mused on the source of all the hatred that had invaded the streets and squares of Benghazi, and about Israel. I recognised the flag above the door of the Jewish Agency office, which promoted the immigration of Libyan Jews. They also taught us to defend ourselves in the event of a pogrom, like that of 1945, when 250 Jews were killed and 3000 injured. But all this I only half-knew in the darkness of the Capua dormitory. What was the connection between us and Israel – the Jews, the Luzon family, us children – myself, Raphael? It had never crossed our minds, as Libyan Jews in Benghazi, to emigrate to Israel. I thought of the stories of my father's grandfather, who fought in Misrata with Ramadan al-Swehli for the independence of Libya. A Jewish patriot! I was looking for answers, even though the questions were not clear. My visions were like silent movies without captions.

After a few weeks, my mother noticed that I was feeding myself with the memories and not with the food provided. I was slowly wasting away. However, the camp imprisonment was more indigestible than the bad food. My mother tried to persuade me to eat, feeding me at every meal. She cried and got angry, beating her breast. Her efforts were to no avail. One night, while everyone was sleeping, she approached my father, took his arms and stared into his eyes, and with a calm, assertive tone she said, 'Come, we will leave for Rome, now.'

Chapter Twelve

After saying our silent goodbyes to the other families, some of whom had been there for months, we left with some of our belongings. We walked to the bus stop for what felt like an eternity. When we arrived, my sisters and I pondered what our parents were thinking during the heated silence. We were revelling in this new-found freedom from the camp, but our feelings had to remain locked up, as we were about to move further into the unknown.

The bus took us to Naples, and from there we were heading to Rome by train. I felt that the passengers on the train were staring with stern, suspicious looks, but Rita, Betty and I were on our best behaviour, thinking this would deter the hostile glances. I turned my head to the window, where I saw the green fields and the rolling hills. Soon my eyelids became heavy and I took a nap.

Once we reached Rome, we walked up to the old Jewish ghetto. We were told that there was a hotel run by Jews, where we could rent a room for a short period. Luckily, my father had some money in an Italian bank, which he had stashed on a previous holiday in Italy.

The Hotel Carmel was small, simple and clean. Since it was close to the ghetto's synagogue and among the Jewish community, we were satisfied with our location. We were in two rooms, our parents in one and Grandma sharing with us three.

'I'm going to look for a flat,' my father said. We remained in our room, frightened to venture out alone. When we woke up the next morning, we found that father was already out again, looking for a new place to live.

A few days later, he found a flat in Via Palestro, away from the synagogue and near Piazza Bologna, where many Jewish refugee families already lived. Since it was only a temporary transition, my mother thought it was unnecessary to furnish, as she was sure we would never survive in that sort of solitude. Father's efforts paid off and eventually he found us a first-floor flat in Via Ciociaria.

We gradually got used to our new flat. The odd smells soon seemed normal, as did the noise from our neighbours and the view from our window. Soon Benghazi became our past and Rome was our present and our future.

We lived close to the rest of the Libyan Jewish community, many of whom were from Tripoli. We'd all meet in the evening in the garden of Piazza Bologna, sitting on benches or standing in small clusters, smoking and talking in Arabic well into the night. Debates would erupt on the subject of Israel, the Six Day War's aftermath and the existing threat of a pogrom. 'King Idris didn't defend us,' some would argue and others would repeat their own version of events for the umpteenth time, while some railed against Muslim neighbours who turned on them, and those who joined the mobs in the streets of Benghazi and Tripoli. There was never a consensus; everyone's recollections were different.

There would often be a Muslim visitor from Libya to see friends. Maybe it was out of guilt or maybe they were on business. We would all crowd around him and hear about events in Libya. We would listen attentively, in silence. When the speaker paused for a while, questions would arise from all sides with a tone of urgency, anxiety and hope. My father used to beg for information about his family in Tripoli. Sometimes the visitor replied that he didn't know, sometimes he remained silent. Sometimes he pretended he didn't hear.

Chapter Thirteen

Grandmother Urida, a lady weighed down by years in both body and soul, sat in front of the Kabbalist in a dark room. The gaunt man with sunken eyes listened to her while she spoke of her son.

'Where is my son? What happened to his family?' she asked anxiously. The Kabbalist asked the names of the missing relatives. 'My son Shalom,' responded Urida, 'Zakya his wife, his children: Raphael, David, Joseph, Abraham, and Ariel.' The man read an amulet, and a piece of parchment with a close eye.

'I'm sorry, ma'am. They're all dead, except for one son. He converted to Islam and remains alive.'

Grandmother Urida moaned, and put a hand to her heart. She then took a small purse from her bag, and handed it to the Kabbalist's assistant lurking in the shadows near a wall. As she stepped out of the building, Israel's merciless sun flooded over her. There will never be certainty until they find a body, she thought, until there is a funeral. A mother doesn't abandon a child when there's still hope.

My father and his brother visited Skata, the former Libyan ambassador in Italy. He looked my father and uncle straight in the eye before reaching behind the desk and revealing a gun. He placed it in front of them, facing the barrel towards himself.

'I know nothing about your brother or his family!' he said in a firm tone.

'Shoot me if you want! Come on, shoot me! I have no news of your brother, understand?'

It soon became apparent what had happened. Officer al-Gritli broke the door of the house and burst in with his men. The whole family were forced into a truck and taken to a place called Sawani Benhadam, Tripoli. Al-Gritli ordered the soldiers to shoot them, but they refused. All of a sudden, he drew his pistol and murdered them, one by one.

In 1993, Raffaello Fellah, a great man and leader within our community, travelled to Libya to meet Gaddafi, and inquire about the Luzon family's fate. Gaddafi was aware of the massacre and said al-Gritli had been arrested. He added that if reparations were granted for Libyan Jews, the family would be the first to benefit. Raffaello then asked where the dead had been buried. Gaddafi revealed they had been placed behind the Muslim cemetery, near the cement factory. It was Raffaello's wish to find the bodies in order to hold a burial, or at least a remembrance ceremony. Unsurprisingly, the wish was never granted. The bodies were in a mass grave, along with victims of Gaddafi's tyrannical regime.

Al-Gritli was put on trial and ended up in prison. However, it was rumoured that he was released in the mid-90s. Some said he'd gone mad and wandered the streets of Tripoli clad in dirty rags. Who knows where the truth lies, but one thing is for certain – Shalom, Zakya, Raffaele, David, Joseph, Abraham and Ariel were no more, but their souls hadn't been swallowed up by Libya, they had reached heaven. May their memory be blessed.

Chapter Fourteen

The Franciscan priests were great teachers who taught us at Freres School La Salle. They were severe, with no tolerance of slackers, but they preapared us to face the world through education and discipline. For many years former students remembered the days passed on the benches of La Salle with gratitude. We would seek each other out like old soldiers gathering to reminisce about the war.

Thanks to the Franciscan priests, I had no problem following my new school's lessons in Italian. Soon, we Libyan students were top of the class. Maybe this was the reason why we were bullied by the native Roman Jews.

Secretly in class, publicly in the hallways and outside on the street, we were bullied and always ended up in fights. 'Go back to Africa! Go back to the jungle!' they'd shout. I suffered abuse, but was too young to reciprocate, burying everything inside me.

I was distressed at how Jews were treating Jews, humiliating those who had been driven from their own countries. I couldn't find a way to express myself apart from fighting back, and then I would usually come off worse. One day I came home and burst into tears as if my body could no longer take the suffering. I told my father everything, and the next morning he came into school with me to see the headmaster. He immediately began to cry with anger, as the headmaster looked on with guilt. All the bitterness and rage that had been bottled up for too long was finding its release.

'This should end immediately or I will go to the police and sue you!' my father shouted before slamming the door, pulling my hand tightly behind him.

The principal came into our class and gave a speech that was initially hard and indignant, but then became sweet and heart felt, concluding: 'We are all Jews, we are all brothers.'

At my desk I finally felt protected and reassured, but at the same time I couldn't help but notice that his words were laced with mistrust, as if he didn't really believe what he was saying.

The insults and fights almost ceased completely and slowly we integrated with the rest of the class, but we were never really friends, and the Libyans stayed together until the first marriage celebration between a Libyan Jew and a Roman Jew.

Chapter Fifteen

I studied at a private high school, as my father didn't want me to study on Shabbat, and in order to pay the fees, he worked as the school's accountant. I was well accepted among the other students, albeit with curiosity. They often wanted to know more about Libya and about my journey to Italy. After completing high school, I attended university while working in a shop. I would attend synagogue on a Friday night with my father, who still sang the prayers, like back in Benghazi. It seemed to transport him back home as he sang with his eyes closed.

One day Raffaello Fellah met my father in the street. Their eyes were so different. My father's eyes were dimmed, compared to the glittering eyes of Raffaello, who had the look of a leader.

Maybe Raffaello knew of my father's anguish and wanted to offer assistance, or maybe he really needed a helping hand and an employee. Raffaello Fellah had undertaken the difficult task of preserving our traditions, as the founder of The Association of Jews Born in Libya and the Libyan Jewish Support Committee. With a team of others, he established a synagogue in a small flat, the first in Via Garfagnana. Later, the synagogue of Beth Hel was established in a former cinema in Via Padova. Today there are four synagogues with cultural activities in full swing, all thanks to Raffaello's efforts. He dedicated his whole life to preserving our culture, which was shattered by war and conflict.

He organised conferences on the history of Libyan Jews, promoted the writing of books and documentary productions, brought together exiled Libyan Jews from around the world and maintained contacts with the Libyan government – even Colonel Gaddafi – to be in touch with our past and to investigate the fate of all those left behind. Raffaello Fellah's activities brought us momentary hope for a reconciliation between Libya and its Jewish community.

Raffaello Fellah asked my father whether I would be able to assist him at work. A few days later I teamed up with him, and began working ten hours a day for a pittance. However, the education he gave me was priceless, especially when observing his great ability to establish relationships with people, to convey respect and gratification while remaining authoritative. He would refer to me as his 'right-hand man' and that alone was a sufficient reward for all my efforts. Even though I started working at the Israeli Embassy, I remain connected to Raffaello on all his projects.

Today I carry his ideas and values in my preservation work for the Jewish Libyan diaspora. When I am challenged by the bleakness of life, I recollect Raffaello's determined face. His very own father was murdered in the 1945 Tripoli pogroms, yet I had never heard him speak an abusive or offensive word against the Muslims in Libya. He never tired of saying that we shouldn't impose collective guilt, as there are many good people among the killers and plunderers. I always tried to follow his principles.

Fiammetta

Pain is a certainty but suffering is optional in this life. I have often repeated this phrase, but it wasn't so easy after the death of Fiammetta. I loved her when she, still a young girl, was one of the leaders of Rome's chapter of Shomer Ha'tza'ir, the socialist Jewish youth movement. However, I couldn't see any affection for me in her eyes, and eventually she travelled to discover other countries, working as a guide at holiday villages, before spending time in Israel.

When she returned to Italy, I met her at a mutual friend's party. The same big, curious eyes and broad smile, her skin soft as silk. After seeing her, it took me no time to resume my courtship. I told her that I would be travelling to Florence with an American friend. It was true, but I wanted to make her jealous. After returning from the short trip, we went out together and she expressed her wish to see Florence one day, insisting I should take her there. Her words opened the gates of our love, and we married on 21 October 1990, followed by a long honeymoon trip to Indonesia, Thailand and Singapore, where I discovered a woman full of enthusiasm, eager to try everything in the world, independent and with a wonderful sense of humour. We lived happily together; I worked at the embassy and she worked as a tour guide. Soon after, she became pregnant.

She arranged a big party on my birthday and we felt honoured to receive an Israeli foreign minister, who joined the party. The party went on till late; we enjoyed singing songs and exchanging anecdotes. The very next day, Fiammetta fainted and was hospitalised. The doctors said that it was pregnancy-related. On 18 July our daughter Gaia was born, filling our hearts with happiness. But within a week Fiammetta had an epileptic fit and collapsed. After various examinations she was diagnosed with a brain tumour. Doctors said she had two months to live.

I couldn't take it in and the devastating news failed to stir a reaction in me. I phoned Ambassador Drori and, with his help, we sent all her medical records to Hadassah Hospital, Jerusalem. They asked us to fly there immediately for surgery. The expenses amounted to $180,000. Libyan and Roman Jews supported us by providing a third of the total costs. We received assistance from the Italian Jews in Jerusalem, especially Emanuele Corinaldi, blessed be his memory, and his wife Zina, and also Nava Amikam Levi, Shoham Einav, Lea Cohen, Benjamin Lazar, Yaakov Teshuba, as well as the Israeli government. They all supported us and prayed for Fiammetta.

The operation left her paralysed on the left side of her body, but she was alive. Prolonged rehabilitation started and we faced both psychological and economic difficulties. Little Gaia was raised by my mother and sisters.

To make matters worse, Fiammetta was diagnosed with cancer again. Despite suffering financially, we returned to Israel, where she underwent another operation. I was sitting next to her while she battled for her life in bed, drifting in and out of consciousness. When I grabbed her hand, with great effort she turned her head to look into my eyes, saying, 'Promise me you will raise Gaia in Israel.' She passed away on 17 October 1992, the day of the feast of Sukkot. The funeral was postponed till 21 October, our second wedding anniversary.

Rav Madar had thick glasses, a black hat and a striped jacket. Sunlight glinted off the shovel, forcing me to look away. When I looked at him again he had already sunk the shovel into the earth, digging until the pit was big enough. He then grabbed a small tree and planted it. Next, he covered the hole and flattened the earth at the base of the tree, and then recited the blessing of the trees, Birkat ha'ilanot.

All the families go to the Bosco Olitorio in the early hours of the morning. We camped there, as the Jews of the Exodus in the desert did. It's a huge party. I ran with the other children among the trees, jumping over the tablecloths which had been laid on the ground. I held a knaak tightly, a biscuit made of eggs, flour, sugar and orange blossom. Around me there was a collective picnic, like a huge chessboard on the ground covered with needles, leaves and grass. Everyone ate and told stories, eating Lubia bel Kemmun, a sour stew made of beans, cumin, chilli and mrosia, with apricots. Time passed and our community felt alive, enjoying the fertility of the land. My father stood up, and in a powerful voice sang the first song of the party, with everyone joining in and clapping their hands.

Chapter Sixteen

When I filled in the documents needed for my emigration to Israel, my heart was filled with emotion and my hands were trembling while signing the papers. I realised that I was approaching an untold old dream. The preparations were long and tiring, but on a spring evening my friends and relatives arrived at our home to say goodbye to us. The next morning Gaia and I left. In Israel we met my grandmother Urida, who had moved there a few years before, and many of my cousins. We were not left alone; I was overcome with a strange sense of excitement, almost euphoria, tempered by a veil of sadness over this special joyful moment. We started a new life, but twenty-eight years of my life spent in Rome had come to an end.

We arrived at Tel Aviv's Ben Gurion airport. Along with other immigrants, we were led to a small room to fill in the forms. 'When will we receive identity cards?' was the first thing I asked the clerk who helped us.

'Soon,' he responded dryly, giving me my first lesson in Israeli bluntness. Outside the airport we found our relatives waiting for us. They welcomed us with applause, hugs and kisses. We travelled to Bat Yam, where we rented a flat so small that it was soon full up with our belongings alone. Being tired, we slept on our new beds. The next morning at dawn I woke up and realised that I was in Israel. I in a state of euphoria, where every single gesture of mine seemed like a miracle. I went out to buy milk and rejoiced at the fact that I was buying milk in Israel; people in the street said 'hello' to me and I smiled with happiness as the word was addressed to me in Hebrew; I walked the streets with a halo of satisfaction, as if I had achieved enlightenment.

The euphoria only lasted for about two weeks. I realised that soon I must find a job to ensure a dignified life for myself and for my daughter, and I was confident. Before travelling to Israel, I met many influential people at the embassy, and they had all promised me that they would not hesitate to help me once I arrived; that, in fact, it would be their pleasure. I soon discovered that no one wanted to, or maybe no one could, help me in that regard. All my requests for referrals were met with silence. Eventually, reality took over and the euphoria was slowly replaced by a deep bitterness and a sense of betrayal.

Finally, thanks to a friend of my mother, I was given a post as director in a nursing home. Though it was a simple job, for a year and a half I invested all my efforts into making a better life for the residents. I did not consider them as people battling for their life or people to be pitied. Instead these people were rich with experience and history, people from whom I could learn something. They deserved my respect. It was during my time at the nursing home that I heard that prime minister Yitzhak Rabin had been assassinated.

Chapter Seventeen

Tel Aviv, 5 November 1995

On that particular night, I went for a late walk, looking at the stars filling the whole sky. I was aware of the shadows of cars and trees, a cat crossing the road; barely a breath of wind. It was heavy with a strange silence. Suddenly, I heard my mobile ringing in my pocket. It was my friend Amos Leghziel, a news photographer.

'Raphael, did you hear?'

'What?'

'Someone shot Rabin.'

A great void suddenly opened up inside me, filled with a sense of disorientation. My words were wedged in my throat as I tried to digest the news. Before having a chance to reply, I was called by the TG1 news channel from Rome: 'Listen, RAI needs someone to tell us what's going on there. Can you do it?'

I accepted without hesitation and in no time I was live on TV for four hours, almost without stopping, except to recharge my phone. I spoke to the Italian nation, but I also had to speak to myself in an attempt to process this news, to make sense, to understand the reason for this madness, to imagine the consequences of this murderous fanatic's actions. I described the scenes, the outcry and the desperation of the people on the streets; the anguish that accelerated by the hour at the fear of losing the man who was considered most precious to the people of Israel – a leader who might have been able to finally bring peace. I had a sudden realisation later that night

– this was my calling. I was put on this planet to promote the goodness of humanity and peace between faiths.

I continued contextualising the Israeli situation to the Italians until my voice was hoarse. Next, the news channel switched to a man in a doctor's jacket, looking very haunted: 'Yitzhak Rabin is dead,' he told the world.

A day of mourning began the next day. The director of RAI 1 called to thank me for the impromptu broadcast the previous night. He explained that RAI didn't have a branch in Israel and, to my surprise, he asked me to establish one and work for them. A new period of responsibility had begun, but the death of Rabin remained engraved in my heart with fire, changing me forever. Every time a new attack shook the foundations of Israel, blood and pain were shed by its people and I was preparing for yet another broadcast. Images of that night would always return. The future was now evolving into a grim reality.

Hana

Rav Amar, a *zaddik* and *mekubal*, a wise rabbi who could see into the heart and understand one's needs, despite being blind. This didn't prevent him from introducing me to a woman named Hana. He called me on the phone and cheerfully told me, 'Raphael, yesterday I was at a circumcision ceremony and I met your wife.' I hated the idea of arranged marriages and I didn't want to meet this woman. But at the same time, I didn't want to disappoint Rav Amar.

As soon as I saw her, I was overcome with a clear and mysterious feeling of relaxation, calmness, serenity and strength. Love didn't spark immediately. Meanwhile, Rav Amar would repeatedly urge me not to linger, saying that Hana was the right woman for me.

A widower who has got used to living alone with a daughter finds it difficult to change their life. The idea of awakening feelings of the past is daunting, to say the least. In the end, her smile and kind eyes helped me find the courage to start a new life, and I persuaded her to join me. Maybe we were just soulmates, as Rav Amar had said. I realised that one day while sitting on a plane in Tel Aviv, waiting to disembark. A longing to see her exploded within me. I wanted to hold her, as if I had suddenly realised that I couldn't live without her. I got off the plane, took a taxi and went directly to her house with my heart hammering.

Then we got married on 25 May 2000. The marriage was performed by Rabbis Amar and Pinto. At last I had found a true companion in my wife, a woman who showed motherly love to my daughter Gaia and with whom I have always been happy.

A few months later Rav Amar passed away. May his memory be blessed.

Pinto was also a man of great wisdom and a *mekubal*. He had been a great inspiration for my inner peace and I used to meet him regularly to confide my moods and receive words of comfort. Rav Pinto, who hails from a family of great Kabbalists, has witnessed miraculous events. One of them concerned me in particular.

I underwent surgery to remove a deposit of fat from my neck, which was usually a simple operation. However, the doctor made a mistake and caused a haemorrhage, which nearly killed me. The surgical team performed a tracheotomy and I was in intensive care for a long time. One day, the doctor came into my hospital room, wearing a serious expression. He told me that the tubes would be removed after two months, and I would need to talk through a device held against my throat, which unavoidably distorts the voice. The voice! I was a television correspondent and the voice was my crucial tool. I was also a singer in the synagogue like my father, and my voice gave me spiritual strength. I fell into despair on hearing the doctor's words.

I called my sister to inform Rav Pinto. He reached me within an hour, accompanied by Rabbi Yitzhak, his assistant, carrying a Torah scroll. They recited the psalms in the hospital room. I listened to them without knowing how to react. When they finished, Rav Pinto greeted me warmly and asked me to call the next day.

The next morning, the doctor visited me with the report in his hand. He said that something had gone wrong during the previous examination. Without warning, he pulled the tube out of my throat, plugging the hole with his hand.

'How are you feeling?' he asked.

'Fine, thank God,' I said.

He simply said that I could go home in a few days. Immediately I called my mother, who burst into tears. Then I called Rav Pinto, who laughed and said, 'You thought that I wasn't being serious yesterday when I asked you to call me, is that right?'

Chapter Eighteen

I left my job at RAI and co-founded an organisation called Jubillenium with some others. The mission was to promote the mutual understanding and solidarity of the monotheistic religions. I had the opportunity to meet people of great charisma and spirituality, including priests, imams and rabbis, intellectual Muslims and Jews, as well as both Israeli and Palestinian politicians. I always tried to touch the heart with my sincere ideas. I believe that no grudges could last forever and that reconciliation is always possible, that a 'no' can become a 'yes' only if we want it to. I attended various conferences and meetings, and had the opportunity to meet the Dalai Lama, a man full of human warmth. He turned to me and my daughter Gaia as if we were his brother and sister. We felt his attention, despite being only two among the countless people.

As a representative of the Jubillenium group, I met Pope John Paul II during a trip to Vatican City. He made a huge impression on me. Not for the papal robes he wore or the elevating environment. It was his aura, which emanated the wisdom of a wise man. My memories associated with the Dalai Lama came to the fore, as if these two men were inhabited by the same spirit of light.

We had come to Vatican City to present our programme of events in view of the Millennium Jubilee and the Pope's visit to Israel. I began to address His Holiness with a certain awe: 'We thought that the events taking place in the Holy Land ...'

John Paul II interrupted me with a smile. 'In Israel!' I had naively thought it would be better to speak as a Catholic, but the Pope in his wisdom and sense of humour answered me as a Jew.

For me it was an exciting period, but it was soon over and I was left jobless. Circumstances dictated that I should accept an invitation from some cousins in the United Kingdom and, together with my daughter Gaia, I moved to London.

To our right was the sea, to our left the Sahara Desert. The bus rented by my father travelled along the coastal road as the sun began to heat the asphalt. Exactly halfway between Benghazi and Tripoli we passed under El Gauss, the arch built by Italians in honour of the Fileni brothers, Carthaginian heroes. Later, an arch built by Italo Balbo was erected. He was the man who forced Libyan Jews to open their stores on Shabbat. The Jews had refused, and Balbo had made the Jewish community's élite march naked to the town's central square.

Abandoning Cyrenaica, we passed by Sirte and then Misrata. We stopped for a break in the hot sun to freshen up, drinking lagbi and palm juice. The children gathered around us spoke a different dialect, with a more rounded, gentle pronun-ciation. We gave them sweets. At dusk we arrived in Tripoli, at the home of my grandmother Urida and all my uncles and cousins. We were spending Pesach all together, and celebrating The Seder– Passover evening. We read the Haggadah into the night, the story of the liberation from Egypt, sang traditional songs and enjoyed the ritual meal. Afterwards the smaller children would drift off to sleep in the arms of their parents, as we all lounged on sofas and carpets, slaves no more. My eyelids were already heavy while thinking of the Eighth Day, the last day of the festival, when all the children would enact chiahlit, a small Seder with laden tables, miniature dishes and child-sized chairs, while behind us a few adults sang about liberty, to which we were conducted by our Moses.

Chapter Nineteen

There's nothing more reassuring than the smell of books. This thought often occurred to me as I paced in front of the bookshelves. When there were no customers, especially in the morning hours, I caressed volumes of the Talmud and dwelt upon Jewish history and philosophy books. I could remain by the counter for hours, absorbing the words in suspended time.

After finding a flat in London, I found a position as a clerk in a Jewish library. The days passed with regularity, always culminating in a peaceful Shabbat. Events and places of the past were obscured by a mist, as the London fog would welcome me in the mornings when I headed to work. It was as if my memories were on hold, or supposed to be forgotten, perhaps to be awoken by a sudden storm.

It was a sunny November morning when I heard the noise of the door, followed by light footsteps entering the library. A beautiful girl with olive skin and green eyes came over and asked me if there was a book on the history of Libyan Jews. I courteously asked why she was looking for it. She told me that she was the daughter of an Englishman and a Jewish woman who had fled Libya. I didn't immediately reveal my history, and instead I started my search in the history section. My index finger passed from one title to another, but did not rest on a choice. I was shocked to find no comprehensive account of our recent history. I had a faint hope that perhaps our stock was simply lacking the right book.

The girl and I engaged in a conversation. Her name was Layla. We stood for a long time, exchanging stories. In an attempt to rediscover her roots, she said, she had many friends in London who had been assisted by the Libyan Jewish community to organise visits to the country. We exchanged addresses and promised to stay in touch. When she left the library, I sat at the counter and stared at the piece of paper along with her name, phone number and email. At the time, I knew nothing about email.

I realised that I had been dramatically changed by something. A sudden enthusiasm caught hold of me, with an impatience driven by something. I closed the library an hour early and headed for home. On the way back, despite the bitter cold of winter that froze my cheeks, and surrounded by the red brick walls of London, distant images and half-forgotten landscapes arose, along with faces and phrases, taking me back to those narrow streets of Benghazi's Jewish Quarter. When I reached home, I was breathless and had to stop to collect myself.

As I stepped inside, Hana and Gaia looked at me strangely, noticing some change. I tried to act as though nothing had happened, like a spy hiding a valuable secret. I sat nonchalantly on a chair in the living room. At dinner, I began to tell them about Layla's visit and eventually pulled out the piece of paper.

'She also left me her email address, but I don't know what to do with it.'

'Dad, I'll open a personal email account for you and you can write to whoever you want! And I'll teach you how to use the internet, and to open a Facebook account,' Gaia answered enthusiastically.

Chapter Twenty

Subsequently Layla put me in touch with some Libyan Muslims, some of whom were exiles from the Gaddafi regime. Introduction followed introduction, until meetings became frequent. With the help of Hana, we opened our home to new friends and in time it became a hub for all Libyans in London. Our soirees at home, filled with food, songs and Libyan anecdotes, regularly featured men and women we had never met before. A tight Libyan circle had emerged in London's Hendon. I was elated by this new universe that had blossomed around us.

I started writing articles on the history of my family, the Jewish community in Benghazi, and the relationships between Muslims and Jews. They were published on websites and in Arabic newspapers, and led to further meetings, other discussions – often heated, sometimes even violent – but for me this was intoxicating and each challenge was answered with calm patience. I wanted my words to build a peaceful path for all of us.

I began to reach out online to strangers – Libyans, Israelis, Italians and other Europeans. The majority of Libyan Jews demanded compensation for their losses at the time of their expulsion from Libya in 1967. I further submitted the objective to claim a right of return, and the reacquisition of our social and political rights, as well as our lost property and inheritance.

Among my Facebook contacts, one person in particular struck me immediately: a young girl named Majdouline. During the night I often found it hard to sleep while thinking of the conversations we had during the day. My head was full of plans for conferences on Libyan Judaism and shepherding the formation of the Union of Libyan Jews. The thrill of discovering other Libyan families who had fled from our homeland was gratifying. However, what made me sleepless more than anything else was Israel, one of the most difficult topics to discuss with my Muslim friends. I never gave up trying to narrate the story of Israel and at nights I used to rehearse my future conversations with them.

Ahmed Rahal

Sometimes a special bond arises when you meet someone. A person whose eyes mirror your own reflection with an incredible clarity, where ideals prove to be mutual, even before a friendship is born. It becomes clear with an irrefutable certainty that this person can be trusted.

This is what happened when I met Ahmed Rahal. His eyes were dim with melancholy and he had an air of living in exile, yet he tranquilly upheld his beliefs. Nothing in the world would induce him to abandon his hopes, which happened to coincide with mine: coexistence among people in spite of the turbulent winds of hatred and violence.

He heard my story in silence, listening with tearful eyes and wearing an expression of guilt. Even though it was not his fault, he took some responsibility for what had happened, the violence towards Libyan Jews by the Muslims of Libya. We began to meet often, engaging in long discussions and sharing our stories. Gradually, we realised that our vision of the world and, in particular, the future of Libya, was converging into a single view. We demanded that every piece of our history should be analysed through the magnifying glass of truth and justice. Ahmed had been a writer and a Libyan television journalist. We decided to write a book together in Arabic that would disclose the history of Libya via the threads of coexistence, solidarity and cooperation among the three monotheistic religions – Islam, Judaism and Christianity. We worked for a year collecting material, conducting interviews, writing and rewriting. Finally, the book was ready, and we decided to send a copy to the Libyan embassy in London.

After a few months an embassy official contacted us to inform us that the book had reached the hands of Gaddafi, who had appreciated the work. Further, we received the welcome news that it would be presented at the Tripoli Book Fair. We were proud that our work reached Libyan readers. It seemed that the chance to return to Libya after so many years depended on the reach. However, I harboured some fears about the idea of returning to my native country. The fear of returning now raised many questions that deeply concerned me.

Sometimes I would leaf through our book, to gain confidence in the matter, literally stroking the pages and reading the passages that touched me the most. I felt infused with a new strength, as if I was reading a Psalm of David. Ahmed Rahal dedicated the opening pages to me, and his words touched me deep inside:

Raphael talks about his life in Benghazi, and his face wears an expression of someone who was forced into exile, but who had not ceased to dream of a return to his world, the world of happy children in his beautiful city. This expression stirs emotion in those around him, and the desire to listen attentively to him, to see the nostalgia and tenderness in the tears at the corners of his eyes, and hear the melody of his voice. In the warmth of his breath, there is the kindness of a Libyan man. Raphael talks, and the listener can take note from his words of reproach against the time, people and places. His memories collect in the recesses of the listeners' minds and the fantasies of their hearts; the epic output in exile with his bleeding wounds; and so my feelings meet those of Raphael in order to reach the scene that he describes, to describe with my pen what we have seen together.

Raphael told me about the places where he and his father were born; the Town Hall Square and its surroundings, Omar Almukhtar Mbarak Alsharif, ending on one side via Almukhtar Omar, and on the other the vegetable market via Almahdui.

But Raphael, to show how his heart is deeply rooted in this place and time fro the past, is so determined to speak of his grandfather on his father's side. His grandfather, who he was named after, Raphael Luzon, was known as the Jewish Sheikh of Misrata, his home city. Grandfather Raphael took part in the war against the Italians, alongside Ramad'an Alsuihli, and was later forced to emigrate east to Benghazi. His family followed him and settled there.

Speaking of his grandfather, Raphael told anecdotes about the participation of Libyan Jews fighting against Italian Jews in the war. The Italian Jews were then betrayed by Mussolini and

*later killed by Hitler. He said that from this history you can
understand the great sense of belonging the Jews felt towards
the country of their birth, whether Italy or Libya.*

*In the stories of his grandfather Raphael depicts the figure
of a religious man and a man who is part of Libyan society,
with deep sensitivity, honesty, and a passion for the education
of children.*

Chapter Twenty-One

The phone rang. It was my friend Dogha, a journalist who had published a paper on the history of the Jews of Libya for Gaddafi.

'Raphael? I'm standing next to our brother, the Leader.'

Drops of cold sweat trickled down my temples, seeming as slow as those forty years that separated me from Libya. I thought he might be joking, so I didn't reply.

'Raphael,' continued Dogha, his voice not quite steady, 'The Brother Leader wants you to visit Libya.'

In the background I heard another voice – was it Gaddafi? I realised this wasn't a joke. Maybe I really would be able to visit home after so many years. Yet I didn't know what to say, and my throat appeared to be blocked. Dogha continued: 'But there's one condition, Raphael; you must bring your mother.'

At this, I was able to speak: 'But my mother is old and sick ...'

Before I could finish the sentence, I remembered a phrase of my mother's that I'd included in the article I'd sent: 'I hope not to die before seeing Benghazi, where I was born ...'

'Don't worry, Raphael, there will be a nurse who'll accompany you at all times.'

I could only answer: 'OK, but I have to bring my sister, so she can be with our mother.'

After a pause the request was accepted. With the phone shaking in my hands, I imagined the stern face of Gaddafi nodding in silence.

I collapsed on the sofa breathless, trying to put my thoughts in order. But before I had time to decide who to call first, my phone was ringing again. I was informed that the Libyan Embassy in London had given me permission to travel to Libya and that the tickets had been reserved for the following Monday. Events seemed to be out of control, as if I were no longer in charge. It felt like a gamble. Perhaps it was dangerous; maybe I didn't really know the country anymore. Maybe no one really wanted to welcome a Jew to Libya. Perhaps the whole trip would be a huge disappointment, or worse.

Although I was hesitant at first, in a matter of days my mother, my sister Rita and I embarked on the Air Afriqiyah plane. As we approached the Libyan coast, we peered through the windows, hoping for a glimpse of the land below. Two men sat in silence behind us, listening to our every word. We knew they were our bodyguards. Suddenly, the blue sea cuts to the yellow earth like a memory, leaving us stunned and silent.

We were driven to a luxurious Tripoli hotel, escorted by eight people including agents, policemen and officials, who would accompany us the entire trip. We had just enough time to walk the streets of the Hara, the old Jewish Quarter. Now the area is called the 'Old Town', and the houses had been replaced by small artisan and goldsmith shops, full of jewellery, *deblej*, *chalchal*, and other stalls bursting with spices, fruits and vegetables. The air was full of piquant smells. The colours and sounds were somehow familiar. Portraits of Gaddafi were posted everywhere. Only the beautiful sea remained unchanged and as transparent as the clear sky above. There was something blocking our joy, as if a valve in our hearts had been closed up and sealed. We returned to the hotel early, viewing the modern city full of tall buildings, cafés, tourists, around us. We retired to our rooms with turbulent souls, numbed by this clash with our past. The next morning we travelled to see our home in Benghazi.

We flew to Benghazi with Buraq Air, named after the winged horse that flew the Prophet Mohammed to heaven. When we landed, I immediately requested to visit the old Jewish Quarter in the Omar el-Mukhtar district. Our guides didn't know the way, so we abandoned the car and I led the way on foot, as I recognised the streets from my childhood memories. As I followed the path to my family home, I began to walk faster and faster, and before I knew it I was running. The security entourage began to run too, followed by my mother and sister, who moved a little slower. Whoever saw such a scene would have had to laugh. Nostalgia swept away all feelings of repression; even the suffering, humiliation, expulsion and the insults from all those years ago. My only burning desire was to see our home.

I ran up the stairs as tears flooded my eyes, and looked at the front door, with my mother and Rita stood next to me, weeping. Sadly, the door remained closed despite us returning three times that day. We wanted nothing more than to see the rooms that existed behind the wooden door. We knew nothing had really changed inside, as nothing had changed in the courtyard and front garden. We felt as if the house had been waiting for a final farewell. But the new inhabitants had no compassion and didn't show their faces, probably fearing that we had come to demand our property back. Rather we were there only to heal an old wound, however painful it might be.

We went to Sla el-Kabira, once Benghazi's largest synagogue, which was now a Coptic church. After a short negotiation the priests allowed us inside. The silence of the interior contrasted with my memories of that place, which had been so full of life, community and prayer. It was a different silence – fearful – invading the place that had been so dear to us all. Disoriented, we looked at the walls. The Torah ark, Stars of David, and chandeliers were all replaced with crucifixes and other sacred Christian imagery. We were all overwhelmed with a great sadness, more so than when we stood outside our home.

It felt like a desecration, a symbol of the destruction of our community; the end of two thousand years of Jewish history in Libya. Our silent cries floated through the empty space. Even the officials who accompanied us had glazed eyes as we left the premises, and we received sorrowful glances from the two priests.

We silently made our way to the Souk el-Dalam, a covered market in Benghazi. The early afternoon sun nearly blinded us through the crevices of the last market stall. We then drove to another childhood memory at my request: the Catholic school, La Salle. Again, the driver didn't know the way, so he phoned a friend who had attended my school. I requested that he let me to speak to him as well, as there was a good chance I might know him. As it happened, he had been one of my best friends from school, Dris Abeida, whose father became the governor of Benghazi. He invited us all to dinner that evening.

We reached our former school and once again my sister and I ran. We went down the aisles in search of our classrooms, as our footsteps ricocheted off the tiles, inhaling the school room smells of our past. We ran through the rows of benches inside the rooms. It was as if we had been magically catapulted back in time. Here, under the puzzled eyes of our official minders, were more fragments of our Jewish history. The joy of children had been suddenly awakened! Once again, our demeanour had infected our companions. The visit to La Salle closed the triangle of our identity: the house, the synagogue and the school, three places that moulded me to become a strong, positive individual.

We were scheduled to return to the hotel before dinner, but the school visit had infused me with spirit and energy. I asked to be taken to Jeliana Beach. I'd thought of going there that very morning and was ready with my swimming trunks under my trousers. I undressed at the edge of the beach and after forty years I dived into the beautiful Mediterranean Sea. As I immersed myself, it all really felt like a dream come true – a dream well worth the laughter from the officials and family as I came out of the water dripping wet.

That evening we arrived at the Abeidas' house and received an emotional welcome. Dris and I looked into each other's eyes, one the mirror of the other, taking note of how time had changed us. Internally, it was a pleasant relief, but an emotional one nonetheless. Time had consumed our memories and history.

Dris introduced his mother, explaining that two years before she had suffered a stroke that had virtually paralysed her and she had lost the ability to speak. My mother sat next to her and took her hands in hers, and the two older women looked into each other's eyes. Then, old Rasmia, her eyes two small slits, her black hair wrapped by a green scarf, began to tremble, and with great effort, but clearly, she uttered that single word repeatedly: 'Rachel, Rachel, Rachel ...' The two old women embraced, wrenching tears from us all.

The next day we left Libya with hardly a word said between us. I relived the memories of those days to crystallise them in my mind, convinced that the journey had been like a precious and unique jewel that had come my way by chance.

Chapter Twenty-Two

Ten days had passed since I had returned to London. With 'There must be a mistake,' I stuttered, 'I've already travelled to Libya and returned!' But there was no mistake.

'The Brother Leader wants you to join the anniversary of the Revolution on 1 September.' Full of curiosity, I prepared for the next trip.

I was again welcomed and escorted to a Tripoli hotel by officials. My need for a dialysis session was accommodated at a Tripoli hospital. Before that, however, I was taken to the synagogue of Dar Asrussi, which had recently been restored. On the walls hung photographs of the synagogue before its restoration. As I sat on one of the wooden benches, my thoughts turned to the possibility of reconciliation, even the idea of a Jewish repatriation.

It was the month of Ramadan and the streets were silent, as the sun beamed down. Only at night did the city wake up. The streets were crowded with lights as people celebrated the revolution in the streets.

An officer led me into the Presidential Palace, which was surrounded by guards and soldiers. Hundreds of guests were seated at round tables inside the spacious hall. Among them were ministers, ambassadors and heads of state. I was seated between the ambassadors of Spain and Portugal. During dinner, a folk-dance troupe entertained the guests. At the table next to mine was Moussa Koussa, the notorious intelligence chief, who had just been appointed as the Minister of Foreign Affairs. Our eyes met and stopped long enough that I was compelled to ask him something.

'Do you know me?'

'Raphael Luzon,' he answered, smiling warmly.

And finally, the time came to greet Colonel Gaddafi. I joined the queue and waited my turn. The security minister Abuzed Omar Dorda introduced each guest before the handshake. When it was my turn, once Minister Dorda announced my name, I added, 'Union of the Jews of Libya'. Then Gaddafi asked the minister to have me wait to one side. When he finished all the greetings, he came over. I will always remember his eyes, so black and inscrutable.

'What do you ask of me?' he said.

'The right to return to my home country and the reinstatement of my rights as a Libyan citizen.'

'Don't you want compensation and the return of your property?' he asked.

'Compensation is managed by the Committee of Jews in Libya, chaired by President Shalom Tesciuba. I want to go back to being a citizen of Libya, and I want the truth and justice for the family of my uncle Shalom Luzon, murdered in Tripoli.'

'I never killed any Jews. King Senussi committed those crimes.'

'But you did destroy the Jewish cemeteries of Tripoli and Benghazi,' I replied firmly.

Upon hearing my reply, Minister Dorda turned white.

'What are your immediate demands?' Gaddafi asked.

'I would like to place a plaque on those old cemeteries with the message: "Here lie generations of Jews, who had lived in Libya for more than two thousand years".'

'Write the text and we will create these plaques.'

'And I would like to put up two more plaques. One in front of the mass grave where the bodies of the Raccah Luzon family and other families were thrown, and one in the heart of the Hara, the Jewish Quarter. On the first the names of the members of the families, and on the second the names of all the Jews who died in the pogroms of 1945, 1948 and 1967.'

'Write the text and we will create these plaques.'

'And two last requests,' I added with the last drop of courage, 'I would like to take ten Jews and a rabbi to Tripoli to hold a memorial service in front of the Luzon and Raccah family graves. And I would like to organise a conference at Dar Asrussi, the restored synagogue, a conference on the history of the Jews of Libya and the relationship between the Jews and Muslims, inviting scholars from both faiths.'

'Devise a programme and Minister Dorda will organise the conference. I will sort out the finances.'

These were his last words, after which he turned and left.

Shortly after the outbreak of the February 2011 Revolution, I received a call from Khaled Kaim.

When he was Libya's deputy ambassador in London, he participated in the cultural evenings I held at home. In Libya most of the ministers had already fled, and he was running the Libyan government.

He spoke on behalf of Gaddafi and requested that I come to Libya with other Jews for a conference on coexistence among religions. In effect, he asked me to support Gaddafi.

'In return,' he added, 'you'll immediately be rewarded for all the properties that your family left in Libya.' I asked him to produce a written request in Arabic and English, which arrived a few hours later.

Sitting at our kitchen table, Hana and I looked into each other's eyes.

'The money would allow us to live comfortably.' Those were the only words we exchanged across bitter smiles. In the end, we reached a decision. I responded to Gaddafi in writing, telling him I wasn't for sale. The compensation was too late. I sent a copy of the letter to Mustafa Abdel Jalil, then head of the Revolutionary Committee, but I never received a response.

Chapter Twenty-Three

London, 17 February 2011

Hana and I sat watching the news from Libyan television. The crowds were flaunting the old Libyan flag.

'Look,' I said to my wife. 'They'd prepared this a long time ago, otherwise, when would they have had time to make copies of the flags?'

That evening we had a long, animated discussion on Libya's future with our guests. Among them were many exiles. Later on, some of them joined Abdel Jalil's government, asking me to join them for open discussions.

So for the third time I packed my suitcase and headed for Tripoli. However, this time I didn't revisit the scenes of my past. Now I felt that there was finally a glimmer of future for my country.

I met with entrepreneurs, politicians and old friends to discuss the political situation. Jibril's government garnered a surprising 75 per cent of the vote, but had to rely on all sorts of militias to maintain order and governance. This created a lack of security, to such an extent that wealthy people hid property such as smartphones inside their socks for fear of being attacked. I even saw a man killed during an argument over a parking space.

The country seemed to be at a crossroads, waiting to choose a direction. Soon it became clear to everyone that the direction had been wrong – a path to destruction.

The violence escalated without check, and tens of thousands of civilians were killed as a result. Prisons were filled with people being tortured and Libya was left to its own accord, as the United States and Europe were no longer willing to intervene.

The day before I was set to leave, a discouraging and bleak horizon lay ahead for Libya and its people. Majdouline came to see me in my hotel. She was more beautiful than her Facebook pictures. We sat in the lobby and talked at length about her fight for women's freedom in Libya. She wanted to know all about my history and the history of the Jews of Benghazi and Tripoli. The more I talked, the more she got excited and emotional. I would smile affectionately, as a father would to a daughter. It wouldn't be long before I saw her again.

Just before leaving, I received a phone call from an Israeli journalist. He wanted to come to Libya with a cameraman to shoot a documentary, asking if I could help them obtain a permit. I called on my connections and permission was granted, but with one condition: they must operate under cover of a different nationality.

Chapter Twenty-Four

We met in Rome on 16 July 2012. Emanuel the Israeli journalist and his cameraman Jimmy had Israeli passports, although I'd told them to procure other documents. We didn't want to talk in the tense atmosphere, not even about the planning of the documentary film. The flight seemed longer than usual. Upon arrival I could smile for only one reason: Majdouline was waiting for us, cheerful as always. I requested her as our official translator, though I didn't really need one.

In the hotel we met her friends, all activists of *Haqqi*, meaning 'My Rights', an association for women's rights in the Arab world. We spoke a bit and were photographed together. Jimmy began his first photo shoot, and then I excused myself to go to my room to unpack my suitcase and freshen up. As I lay on the bed, my legs felt heavy and my eyes were dry; however, I checked my phone for emails. Opening my Facebook page, I noticed that the beautiful photos taken in the lobby were already on Majdouline's Facebook profile as well as my own, and beneath it, I could see numerous offensive comments in Arabic.

'They must be whores if they're photographed with a Jew,' one of them said.

Later Emanuel, Jimmy, Majdouline and I set out for Tripoli's Jewish Quarter. Just outside the hotel a bearded man dressed in a kaftan stopped me and asked: 'Who are you? Where are you from?'

I replied in Arabic, 'I'm here to accompany these two journalists for a documentary on Tripoli.'

'It's not true!' said the man, and behind him a boy shouted, 'He is an Israeli from the Mossad. I saw it on television.' We realised that a small crowd was rushing towards us, and the reality of oncoming danger propelled us into our cars. After a few crossings, two military jeeps stopped us. With guns pointing towards us, they ordered us to climb into one of the vehicles. We were taken to a military base, and into a room with only a table and some chairs. An officer arrived and sat at the table, looking directly at each of us. He started slowly, almost reluctantly, asking questions – first name, surname, profession, what are you doing here, why you are interested in Tripoli – until at some point he paused.

Then he sternly asked me, 'What are you doing, Luzon, with two journalists and a video camera on the streets of Tripoli's Jewish Quarter?'

'Is it possible that we've been sitting here for an hour and we haven't even been offered a coffee?!' I answered. The military official smiled and relaxed, as if he had finally recognised that I was his friend. Coffee was served.

'Excuse me,' he confessed at one point in a weak voice. 'I had to do this interview. There are people out there who expect an exemplary punishment for you.'

'And to think that we were all driven out of our country without any money,' I replied, and began opening up about my memories of Libya. Before long we realised that we shared acquaintances and experiences. After the conversation the military official ordered his soldiers to take us back to the hotel. In the jeep we looked at each other and decided that we would go to Benghazi.

Chapter Twenty-Five

Early in the morning we approached the city centre. Emanuel wanted to interview Majdouline and me at famous landmarks. Crossing Maydan Baladya, the Town Hall Square, we realised that some young people were staring at us. Jimmy placed the camera on his shoulder as Emanuel asked me the first question. The young people approached us, shouting for us to turn off the camera. Jimmy pretended to obey, but the camera was still filming. We were driven away, though we tried to pretend nothing had happened.

We ducked into an alley that led towards the cars, trying to mingle with the crowd and cover our tracks. Meanwhile I addressed the crowd in Arabic as they continued to follow us, turning round and trying to convince them that we were journalists. I heard my phone ringing and the voice alarmed us, saying, 'Run away now, away from the Jewish area. They are coming to kill you!' It was the head of the security forces.

'I know ...' I replied, and hung up. Suddenly, we saw the car as we emerged from the shadows of the alley, running. Behind us objects were thrown and we heard a shop shutter lowered loudly. A bottle landed ahead and burst into flames. We managed to reach the car and we drove away at full speed.

I was trying to understand the disaster as my phone beeped. A message from Majdouline: 'Raphael, I was arrested and interrogated. Now they have released me but they are looking for you. Go away!'

My head was empty, my heart was agitated and my kidneys were in pain. Trying to gather my thoughts, all I could think of was my family. Instead of giving me courage, it terrified me because it seemed as if it would be goodbye forever.

I sent a text to Emanuel and Jimmy: 'Danger. Go straight to the airport and take the first flight.' Then I tried scrolling through my contacts for Guido De Sanctis, the Italian Consul General in Benghazi. When I got through to him, I summarised the situation and he told me that he would meet me at the hotel immediately.

I called my friend Simon Bedussa. 'Answer! Answer!' I begged silently.

I heard his voice suddenly: 'Raphael, is everything all right?'

There was only time to say, 'I have a high fever,' and the line dropped. That was our code phrase for danger.

We finally reached the hotel, where I saw Consul De Sanctis. I approached him, but even before we had time to greet each other, a dozen armed men burst into the lobby and dragged me away. The consul tried to intervene, but to no avail. They captured me and threw me into the back of a jeep that skidded away, raising a cloud of dust, through which I saw a young man running in the street shouting for them to stop. Later I found out that he was the son of a friend of Simon, who was trying to protect me.

Two men armed with Kalashnikovs were silent and expressionless. I wondered if this was the end; I wondered how they would kill me. Will I be strangled? I whispered the *Shema* silently and once again I was petrified. However, I told myself that they couldn't assassinate me, as Consul De Sanctis was present at the abduction. They must take this

into account. Then I remembered all the contact information – that of politicians and influential Italians – that I had
left with my mother and sisters before the trip. Surely they
had been notified by Simon, surely they are already spread-
ing the news.

Suddenly the jeep stopped. I was dragged out by a group
of gunmen. They looked at me closely. I had the impression
that they want to sniff me. A man with a dusty beard stepped
forward and breathed heavily on me, asking me what I was
doing in Libya, since I was an Israeli. 'I was born in Libya. It
is my country,' I said.

The questions continued one after another. I spoke in Arabic, trying to answer them all because my salvation might
depend on the ability to weave some kind of relationship
with them.

'Do you prefer Libya or Israel?' one of them asked me.

'Libya is my mother and Israel is my father,' I replied. This
made him laugh.

'And if there is a war, which side are you on?' he insisted.

'I am a pacifist,' I replied. 'I do not fight.'

'He is very cheeky, this Jew,' he said to the other men in
Arabic. All of a sudden, he became silent. The head of the
militia had arrived. He wore a tunic on his head and a *kef-
fiyeh* round his neck. A scar across one eye seemed miraculously intact. His name was al-Haj Abussalam Barghati. He
ordered me to hand over everything, even my watch.

'I would like to call my family,' I requested. Barghati didn't
answer. A soldier grabbed my arm and pushed me towards a
run-down building riddled with bullet holes. It was a prison.
They stopped in front of a cell full of filthy prisoners lying on

the floor. The soldiers made them all come out, screaming and kicking and then pushed me inside. I turned suddenly before they closed the cell.

'I can't sit on this floor. I've just had a kidney transplant!' I screamed. Barghati seemed annoyed, then he made a gesture with his hand. After a few minutes two militants brought a battered chair and set it in the corner. One of them locked the cell.

'I have a flight to London tomorrow,' I said, feeling as if my words were ridiculous in that situation. Barghati replied, with his back to me as he walked away, 'Forget about London.'

I looked down at my dusty shoes, up at the ceiling and then at the stained walls covered in writing. 'God help me,' I whispered as I fell into the chair.

Chapter Twenty-Six

18 July 2012, 19:00

A military camp on the outskirts of Benghazi

I had long ago lost track of time, since they had taken my watch. The Saharan heat permeated from the window cracks, further oppressing the cell's silence, only to be interrupted by the bark of a distant dog. I was alone with my thoughts, left only with the violent cries of prisoners being tortured and interrogated elsewhere in the prison. The thought of death was surprisingly calming. My only worries were about my wife, daughter and two sisters, and the anxiety they must be feeling.

Time passed with the screams of the other detainees being beaten. I had an urge to urinate badly.

'Guard, guard!' a militiaman came to me.

'What do you want?'

'I have to pee.'

'Tough,' he replied.

'I recently had a kidney operation – I need a toilet.' He called another man, who took me to a latrine. My medication would have lasted for three more days, but they had seized all my possessions. Returning to the cell, I asked the militiaman if he could leave the door open, since I suffered from claustrophobia. Surprisingly, they left it ajar. He would return at dawn to close it, before the opening of the prison. The open door aroused mixed feelings in me. On the one hand, it was a relief to have an opening; on the other, I fear edit was a passage to my death.

I lay awake until dawn with memories of the past. Then the door burst open and there stood a man of about sixty years old, dressed in civilian clothing.

'How is the prisoner?' he asked. I decided once again to take on the attitude of the indignant Libyan.

'It's a shame that a son of Benghazi is treated this way! Without food, without a bed and without even my medication! A Libyan patriot who came to celebrate the Revolution!' He assumed a grim expression. Then, angrily he began to shout at the militiamen to bring food immediately and bring him back his suitcase. But I knew that his anger was fake. He was Haj Musa al-Majbari, head of Libyan counter-intelligence. (Two years later he was murdered by Islamic militants, along with his son.)

They served me coffee, biscuits and cheese. Then they took me to an air-conditioned office. I thought things had started to work out, but suddenly the militia swooped into the room and took me back to the cell. One of them whispered in my ear that there was an Italian diplomat asking to see me. I understood that it was De Sanctis. After a few minutes I was taken to him and he began to ask me questions. I was translating into Arabic as we spoke, which annoyed the consul. He told me that we had every right to speak Italian. However, I explained to him that it was better this way, to avoid suspicion.

'Trust me, I'm Libyan, I know the mentality.' Among the militants present, one knew a bit of Italian because he had worked at the port of Genoa. He translated my remarks to the others and they regarded me with looks of appreciation.

'Don't worry, Raphael, the Foreign Ministry has been notified and the situation will be resolved soon. In addition, the
news was broadcasting the Italian and Libyan media. This,
however, has created a problem. It seems a group linked to
al-Qaedaare are looking everywhere for you.'

'For tonight you will stay at my home, and then we'll see,'
interjected Hassan al-Aguri, the deputy head of security.
'Tomorrow Ramadan begins. My wife and my children are
away at my in-laws' house.'

At his home, Hassan al-Aguri prepared dinner for both of
us and allowed me to call my wife and sister. I was able to re-
assure Hana, but Rita demanded to speak to the officer. In a
strong tone she explained my kidney condition. I overheard
her, though muffled, as the man smiled and reassured her.

Chapter Twenty-Seven

I fell asleep right away. A noise came from the kitchen and I awoke startled, but quickly realised that it was Hassan preparing for the first day of Ramadan. The next morning he served me breakfast. I was embarrassed to eat in his house while he was fasting, but he insisted that hospitality is sacred. He was dressed in an elegant *jalabia*, ready to go and pray in the mosque. Before exiting, he grabbed two guns. I followed him, fascinated by his character, strong and calm. While he was praying, I was left in the car with his guards. We had orders not to leave the car for any reason and never to park in one place. The guards asked me if I had any preference of destination. Upon request they drove to the sea – Jeliana Beach, so we were out of town. While we sat in the car, our conversation was so sincere that I forgot everything else. While one of the men was telling a Libyan joke, his mobile rang.

'We have to go,' he said coldly. They took me back to the military base where I waited for De Sanctis, militiamen and Libyan officials.

'We have to find a temporary solution, Raphael,' the consul explained. 'Maybe you have a friend here in Benghazi who could put you up?' I still had many, especially former students from La Salle.

And so, at sunset, I found myself in the car once again, heading for the home of my dear friend, to whom I will be thankful forever. They put me up for several days with the finest hospitality, but nothing could shake my anxiety as I waited for the next step.

I followed the sunset with apprehension, thinking that there was enough time to get to the villa before the Sabbath. At the same time, I couldn't ignore the view and hoped that it would never end.

I stood in front of a beautiful oval table, as I held a glass of grape juice and recited the *kiddush* out loud. I washed my hands to recite the blessing in a marble bathroom and finally recited the blessing over the bread. As I sat down to eat in the silence, the famous Hasidic quote comes to mind: *gam zo l'tovà*–'This too is for the best.'

Every evening at the end of Ramadan, the militia would pick me up from the villa and take me back to the base, where I was interrogated until late at night. The inquisitors changed, as if they all wanted to hear my answers separately. However, the questions were always the same. 'You're not an agent of Mossad?' 'What did Gaddafi want from you?' 'Why did you meet Gaddafi?' 'Tell me every word you heard from Gaddafi.' 'How do you know the journalists?'

All these questions were answered calmly, but after all that repetition, I found solitude in the villa. Consul De Sanctis watched the interrogation. I was never left alone, and I will be forever grateful to him. He filled me in on the ripple of my story in Italy; how many of my friends, Italians and Libyans, were lobbying for my release. He told me about a small event organised by a young Libyan, who had now fled to Tunisia. This young man managed to muster about thirty people via Facebook, and had posted flyers around the main street that read: 'Freedom for Raphael Luzon! Your rights are my rights! Religion is for God, the state is for all.'

All the news, the upheaval, the concern and fear had not broken me. The revelation that a young Libyan had risked his life and rebelled touched me, and I felt my eyes well up with tears.

After seven days the consul came to the villa and told me that the next day we would leave for Italy. I was free.

'But like it is here in Libya, it's not over until it's over,' he added.

'Tonight you'll sleep at my house.'

The next day we set off. There was no plane available. We had to wait three days to board a flight to Istanbul, and then from Istanbul to Rome and from Rome to London. I was free. Thanks to the people for their help, thanks to God and probably a little luck. I hugged my mother, Hana, my daughter Gaia, Rita and Betty, and all the friends to whom I told my story of abduction countless times. Once I was home in our London flat, I finally sat down at the computer, and for the first time I had the feeling of being truly free. I logged into my Facebook page and published a simple post: 'I AM FREE'. And after a few minutes it had received hundreds of 'Likes', and happy comments from friends and strangers – Jews, Muslims and Christians alike.

In the silent streets of Benghazi in the early hours of the day, there were winding lines of men, women and children heading to Labramali Salat, the second largest synagogue in the city. It was the second day of the festival Simchat Torah. Women balanced the jugs of aaffè with zohar and atara, and tea with haranat at either side of the table. Almond pastries, cakes, cookies and potato Burik riiba. And the children held small scrolls of the Torah in their arms and ran around the perimeter of the synagogue between songs, while women threw blessings of confetti and candy into the air amid the cries of the children who try to pick them up. Notables and rabbis were dancing and laughing, singing for the glory of Torah. And every time one of the men ran seven laps, there would be more exuberant jumping; Babi Shimon, Moshe Labi and Amora Dabush hugging and dancing with each other, and even the master Rfali raised his Torah scroll while singing in ecstasy. I was a child, looking on with wide eyes at the feast. Anyone who has never seen the ceremony of Hakafot Shniot of Simchat Torah in Benghazi, well, they don't know what joy is!

Majdouline

Majdouline is sitting in the chair in front of me. She has been with us for two weeks. Tomorrow she will move to an Orthodox Jewish family, to work for them as an au pair. This strong and courageous girl lowers her eyes as she talks about her arrest, torture and humiliation after my exile from Libya. Her eyes are clouded by a veil of sorrow, like a stain in her bright soul. I listen in silence and pray calmly that she will now find happiness. She succeeded in fleeing to Tunis and from there to the UK, where she applied for asylum. I will always help her, I said to myself, as she continues her story. Then she turns to the future: projects and activism for the rights of Arab women. I find myself smiling, now that the veil of sadness over her eyes has lifted and her eyes are shining again.

Epilogue

After the Jews were exiled from the country where they were born, the beating heart of two millennia of Jewish Libya fell silent.

With these lines, I hope my conviction that the good forces inherent in many people will eventually prevail, if we do not lose hope and leave no room for the dark shadows of despair and hatred in our souls. I have come across so much hatred, violence and envy. Men are more like wolves – madness over reason – but still I have witnessed generosity and compassion emerging through the darkness.

I don't know what it is that compels me to seek out good at all costs, to settle differences and to preserve peace among us. A dear friend jokingly answered my question: 'Raphael, you were raised in a religious Jewish family in a Muslim country and you have been educated by priests ... what do you expect?'

I hope that at least one small seed planted during my life grows into a strong, flourishing tree.

Or was it unawareness alone that led me to cross the mine-field of a Libya in the grip of violent Islamic upheaval, even with the risk of brutality or worse. A verse that I often find myself whispering in my heart: 'The Lord will fight for you and ye shall hold your peace' (Exodus 15:14).

Today Libya is isolated and abandoned to violence, at risk of being conquered by Islamic extremism, marred by battles among militias and tribes, and inhabited by a divided and frightened people under an in effective government. The cities are slowly disintegrating and collapsing under mortar fires. Day by day, people are losing hope. Our life span is not enough to heal the wounded souls. So I request of everyone: 'Do not desert Libya.'

Now I am sitting in the living room of my house in London. Hana is here. It is already dark, but we have not turned our lights on. I can see myself from the outside as a body wrapped in darkness. I am shaking my head slightly in bitter frustration at this thought: 'If you had not kicked out your fellow Jews long ago, maybe Libya would now have been different.'

I close my eyes and let my body rest.

Top Left: 27th June 1951 - My parent's wedding day in Benghazi.
Top Right: My grandparents, Raphael and Urida from Misrata.
Bottom: My mother (far right) with other Libyan Jewish women,
Benghazi 1958.

Top: *My class at La Salle School in 1960, Benghazi.*
Left: *My father in his first workplace.*
Right: *Some members of the Luzon family killed in the 1967
pogrom in Tripoli.*

Top: Religious ceremony (Simchat Torah) taking place in Benghazi.
Bottom: Tel Aviv, 1992, with Yizhak Rabin.

Top Left: Meeting the Pope John Paul II in the Vatican, 1999.
Top Right: My daughter Gaia meeting the Dalai Lama.
Bottom: Sitting at the desk of my first class at La Salle, 2010.